AUTHENTIC TRANSCRIPTIONS WITH NOTES AND TABLATURE

SYSTEM OF A

TOXICITY

Music transcriptions by Pete Billmann and Jeff Jacobson

ISBN 0-634-03778-1

HAL•LEONARD®
CORPORATION

7777 W. BLUEMOUND RD. P.O. BOX 13819 MILWAUKEE, WI 53213

Visit Hal Leonard Online at
www.halleonard.com

Photo by Robert Sebree

SYSTEM OF A DOWN
TOXICITY

CONTENTS

Prison Song

Words and Music by Daron Malakian and Serj Tankian

(You and I!) _____

Gtrs. 1 & 2: w/ Rhy. Fig. 1 (1st 3 meas.)

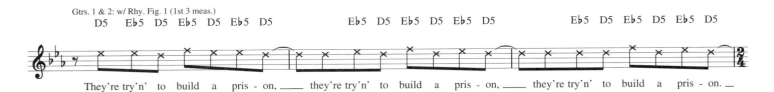

They're try'n' to build a pris - on, _____ they're try'n' to build a pris - on, _____ they're try'n' to build a pris - on. _____

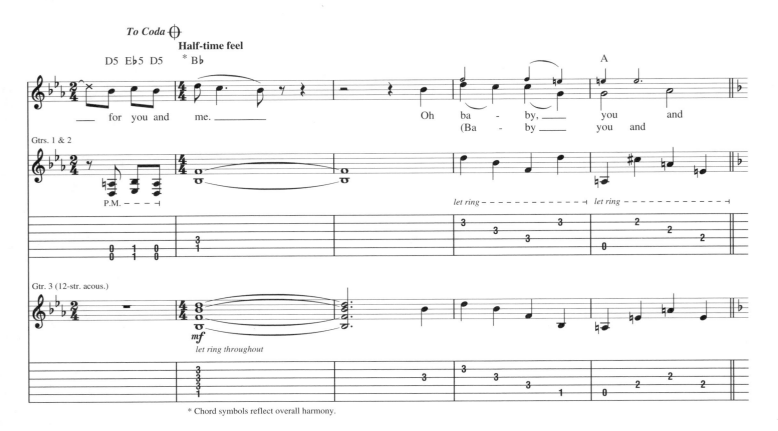

for you and me. _____

Oh ba - by, _____ you and
(Ba - by _____ you and

* Chord symbols reflect overall harmony.

Interlude

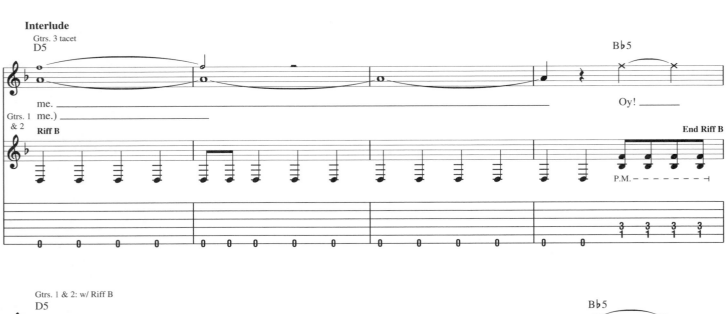

me. _____ Oy! _____

me.) _____

Voy! _____

Voy! _____

Needles

Words and Music by Daron Malakian and Serj Tankian

Drop D tuning, down 1 step:
(low to high) C–G–C–F–A–D

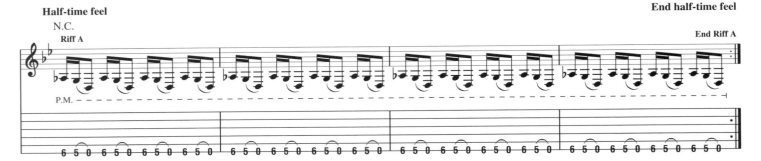

* Doubled throughout

Pull the tape - worm ___ out - of your ass.
(Hey!)
Pull the tape - worm out - of your ass.
(Hey!)

Pull the tape worm out of me.

I'm sit - ting in ___ my room with a nee - dle in ___ my

* Chord symbols reflect implied harmony.

Deer Dance

Words and Music by Daron Malakian and Serj Tankian

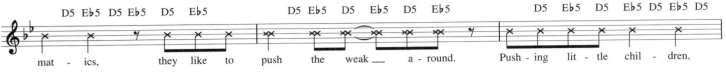

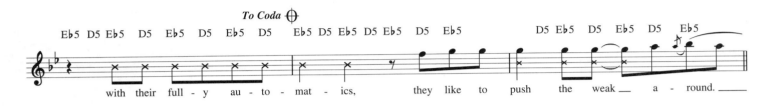

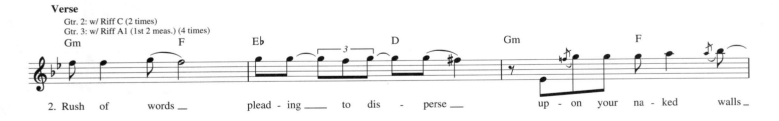

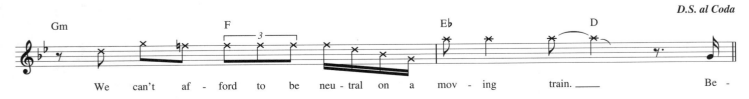

Chorus

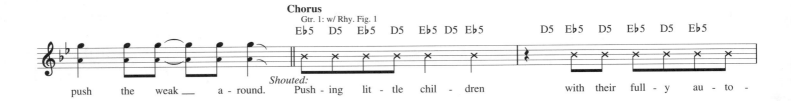

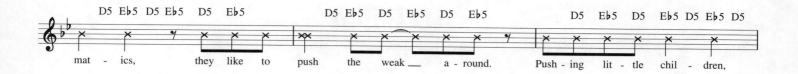

mat - ics, they like to push the weak __ a - round. Push - ing lit - tle chil - dren,

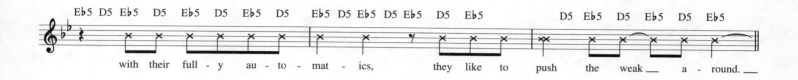

with their full - y au - to - mat - ics, they like to push the weak __ a - round. __

Outro
Half-time feel

_____

Push the weak __ a - round,

Gtr. 1

Rhy. Fig. 2

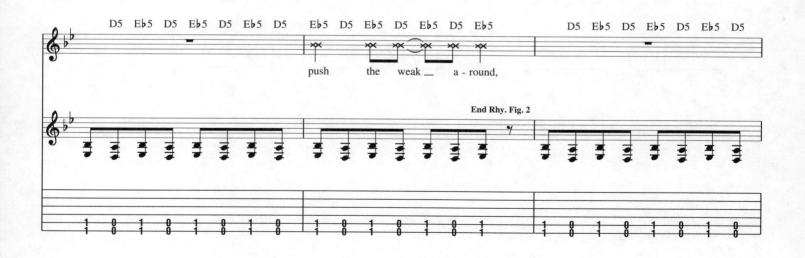

push the weak __ a - round,

End Rhy. Fig. 2

Gtr. 1 w/ Rhy. Fig. 2

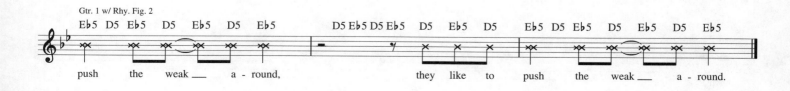

push the weak __ a - round, they like to push the weak __ a - round.

Jet Pilot

Words and Music by Daron Malakian, Serj Tankian and Shavo Odadjian

X

Words and Music by Daron Malakian and Serj Tankian

24

Chop Suey!

Words and Music by Daron Malakian and Serj Tankian

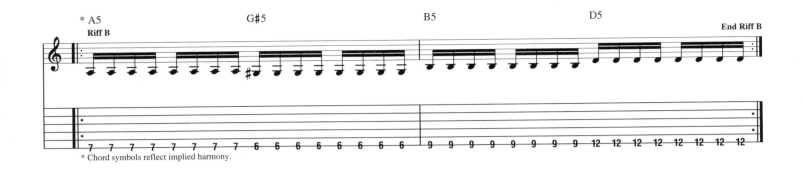

* A5   G#5   B5   D5

End Riff B

Riff B

* Chord symbols reflect implied harmony.

Verse

Bb5 A5 N.C.   Bb5 A5 Bb5 A5 Bb5 A5 Bb5 A5   G#5 N.C.   A5 G#5 A5 G#5 A5 G#5 A5 G#5

1., 2. Wake up,   grab a brush and put a lit-tle make-up.   Hide the scars to fade a-way the

Whispered: (Wake up.

Rhy. Fig. 3   End Rhy. Fig. 3

Gtr. 4: w/ Rhy. Fig. 3 (3 times)

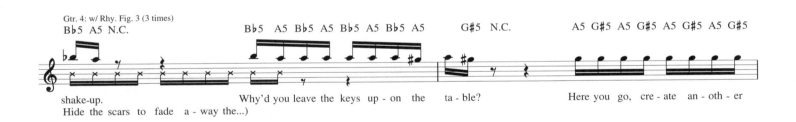

Bb5 A5 N.C.   Bb5 A5 Bb5 A5 Bb5 A5 Bb5 A5   G#5 N.C.   A5 G#5 A5 G#5 A5 G#5 A5 G#5

shake-up.   Why'd you leave the keys up-on the   ta-ble?   Here you go, cre-ate an-oth-er

Hide the scars to fade a-way the...)

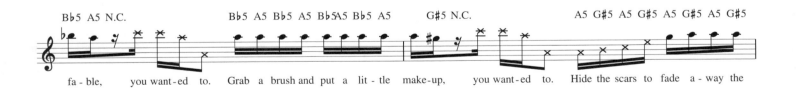

Bb5 A5 N.C.   Bb5 A5 Bb5 A5 Bb5A5 Bb5 A5   G#5 N.C.   A5 G#5 A5 G#5 A5 G#5 A5 G#5

fa-ble,   you want-ed to. Grab a brush and put a lit-tle make-up,   you want-ed to.   Hide the scars to fade a-way the

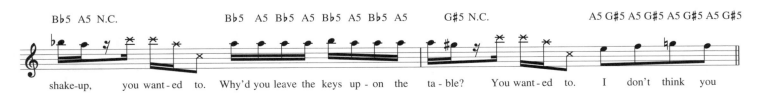

Bb5 A5 N.C.   Bb5 A5 Bb5 A5 Bb5 A5 Bb5 A5   G#5 N.C.   A5 G#5 A5 G#5 A5 G#5 A5 G#5

shake-up,   you want-ed to. Why'd you leave the keys up-on the   ta-ble? You want-ed to.   I   don't think you

Chorus
Half-time feel

trust   in   my   self - right- eous su - i -

cide.____   I   cry___   when an - gels de- serve to ___

End half-time feel
(1st time only)

1.
Interlude
Gtrs. 2 & 4: w/ Rhy. Fig. 2 (2 times)

Bb5 A5 Bb5 A5 Bb5 A5 Bb5 A5   G#5 A5 G#5 A5 G#5 A5 G#5   C5 B5 C5 B5 C5 B5 C5 B5   D5 C5 D5 C5 D5 C5 D5 C5

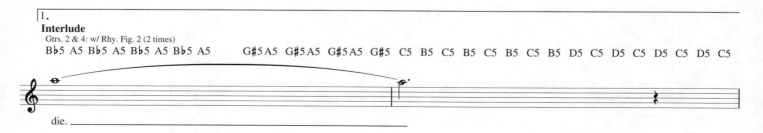

die. _____

Gtrs. 2 & 4: w/ Rhy. Figs. 4 & 4A (4 3/4 times)
Gtr. 3: w/ Riff D

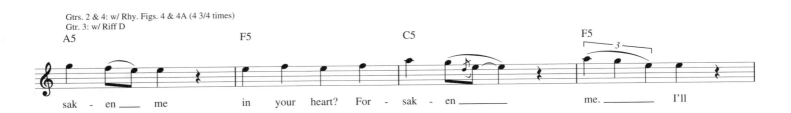

sak - en ___ me in your heart? For - sak - en ___ me. ___ I'll

trust in ___ my ___ self - right - eous su - i - cide. ___

I ___ cry ___ when an - gels de - serve to die ___ in ___

my ___ self - right - eous su - i - cide. ___ I ___ cry ___ when

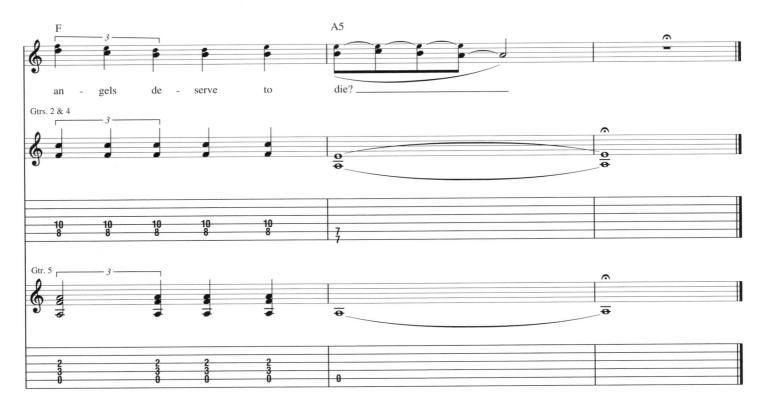

an - gels de - serve to die? ___

Gtrs. 2 & 4

Gtr. 5

Bounce

Words and Music by Daron Malakian, Serj Tankian and Shavo Odadjian

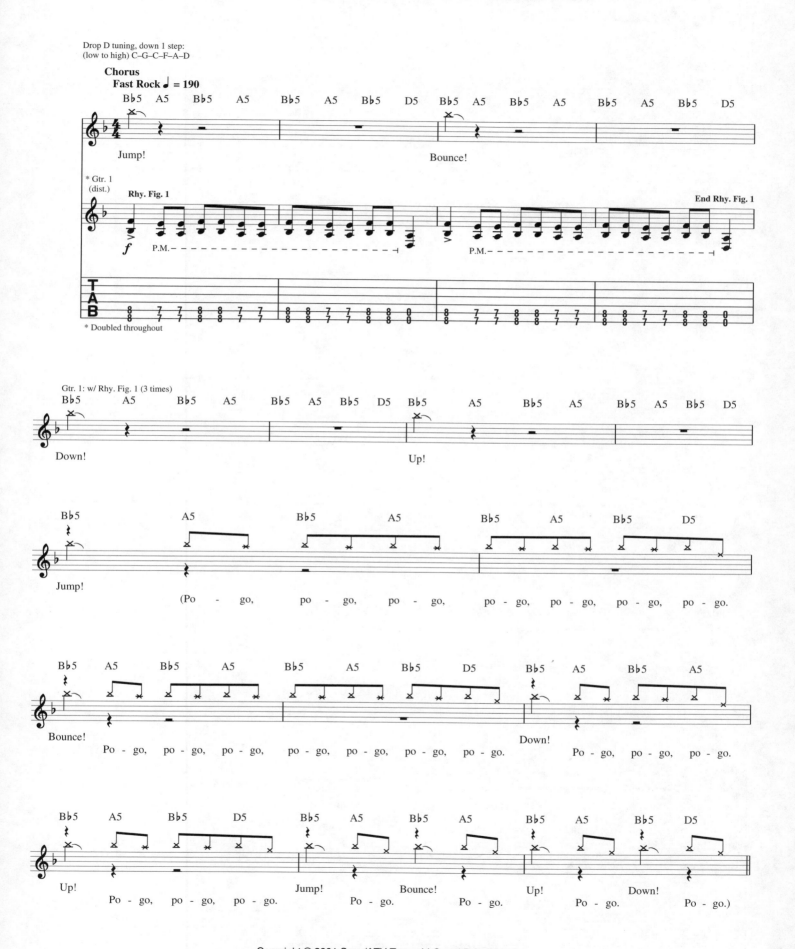

Forest

Words and Music by Daron Malakian and Serj Tankian

39

til the {time end} and make the for- est

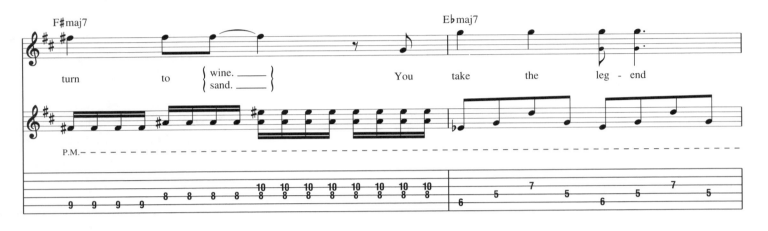

turn to {wine. sand.} You take the leg - end

for a fall. You saw the prod - uct, why can't you see that you

%. **Chorus**
Half-time feel

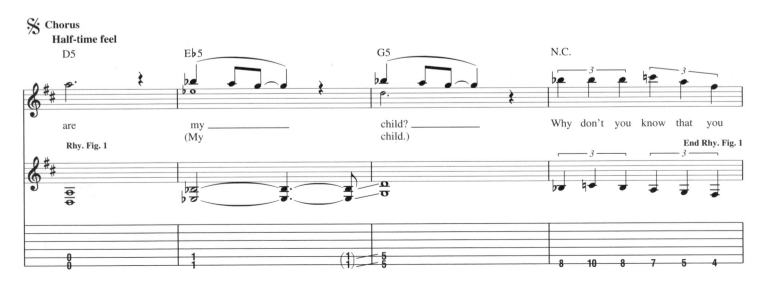

are my child? Why don't you know that you
(My child.)

Verse

Gtr. 2 tacet

** D5/A · · · Eb5/A · · · E5/A · · · F/A · · ·

3. Take this prom-ise for a ride. __ You saw the for-est, now come in-side. ____ You

* Gtr. 3 **Riff A** — **End Riff A**

mp

```
5 0 5 0 5 0 5 0    6 0 6 0 6 0 6 0    7 0 7 0 7 0 7 0    8 0 8 0 8 0 8 0
```

* Bass arr. for gtr.

** Chord symbols reflect implied harmony.

Gtr. 3: w/ Riff A

D5/A · · · Eb5/A · · · E5/A · · · F/A · · ·

took __ the leg-end for it's fall. __ You saw the prod-uct of it all. ____ No

Dmaj7 · · · Ebmaj7 · · · Emaj7 · · · Fmaj7 · · ·

tel-e-vi-sions in the air, __ no cir-cum-ci-sions on the chair. __ You

Gtr. 1

P.M. —

```
       6           6            7           7           8           8           9           9
    4     4     4              5     5     5          6     6     6          7     7     7
 5                          5                       7                    8                8
```

Dmaj7 · · · Ebmaj7 · · ·

made the weap-ons for us all. ____ Just

P.M. — — — — — — — — — — — —

```
         6 6            6 6               7 7           7 7
    4 4        4 4               5 5  5 5       5 5  5 5
 5 5     5 5            5 5      6 6                6 6
```

D.S. al Coda

Emaj7 · · · _3_ · · · Gtr. 1 tacet N.C. · · · _3_ · · · _3_

look at us now! Why can't you see that you

Gtr. 2 _3_ · · · _3_

P.M. — — — — —

```
 7 7      6 6            6 6      7 7      6 6  6 6      8 10    8    7   5   4
       7 7         6 6                7 7          8 8 8 8
```

43

⊕ Coda

ATWA

Words and Music by Daron Malakian and Serj Tankian

Science

Words and Music by Daron Malakian and Serj Tankian

our moth - er earth. _____ 2. Sci -

Verse

- ence fails to rec - og - nize _____ the sin - gle most po -

- tent el - e - ment of hu - man ex - ist - ence. Let - ting the reigns go, to _____

_____ the un - fold - ing is faith, _____ faith, _____ faith, _____ faith. _____ Sci -

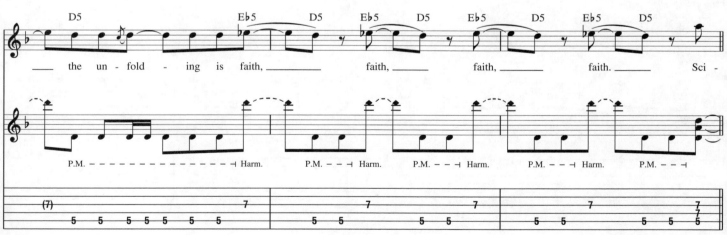

Chorus

Gtrs. 1 & 2: w/ Rhy. Fig. 1 (1 3/4 times)

ence has failed _____ our world. _____ Sci -

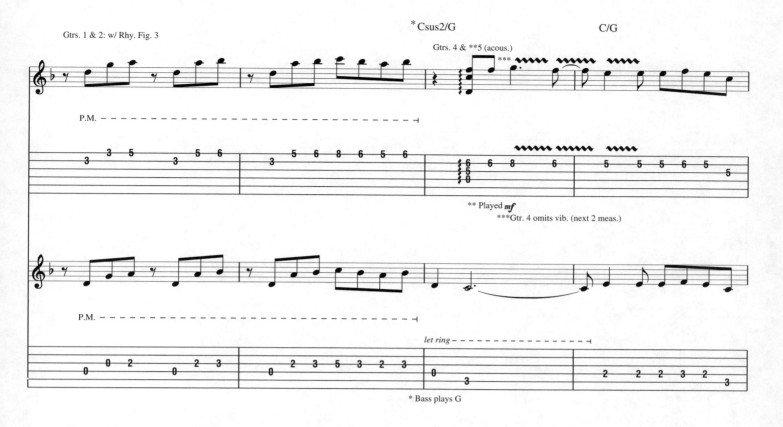

Coda

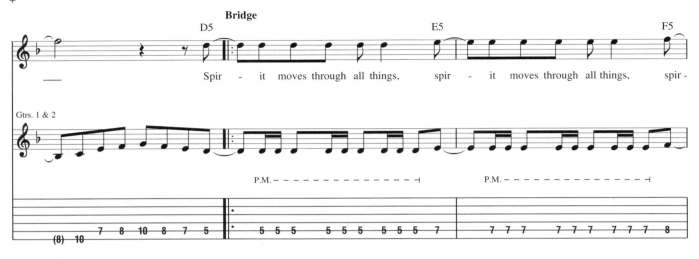

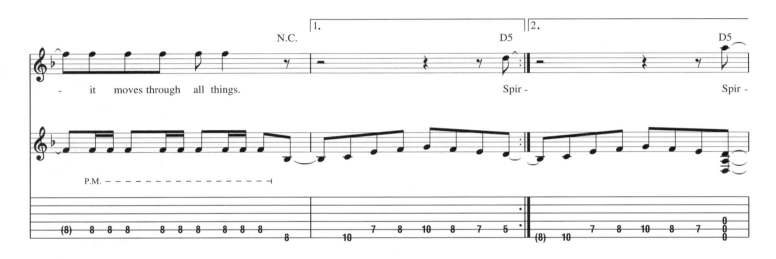

Half-time feel

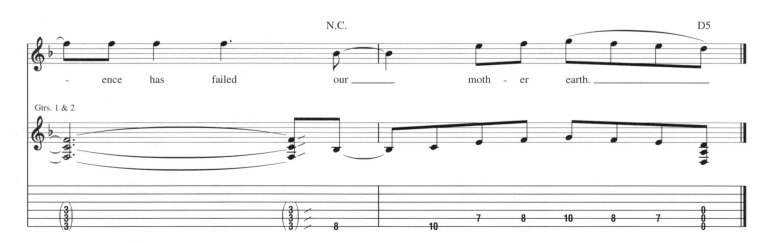

Shimmy

Words and Music by Daron Malakian and Serj Tankian

58

me, _____ I want a house and a wife. _ I wan-na shim-my, shim-my, shim-my through the break of dawn, _ yeah. _

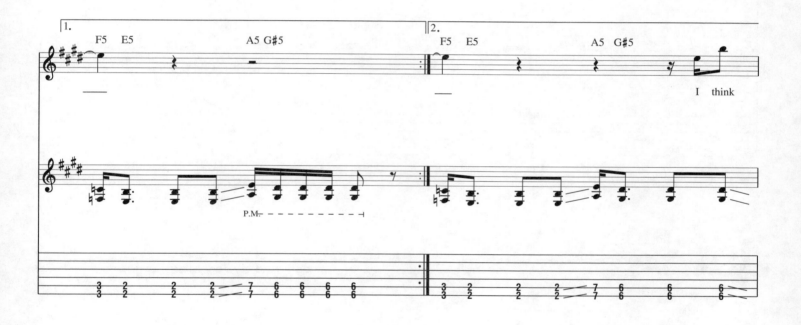

me, _____ I want life. __ I think me, _____ I want a house and a wife. _ I wan-na

shim - my, shim - my, shim - my through the break of dawn, __ yeah. _____ In -

Toxicity

Words and Music by Daron Malakian and Serj Tankian

Drop D tuning, down 1 step:
(low to high) C–G–C–F–A–D

* Gtr. 1: acous.; Gtr. 2: clean elec.
   ** Gtr. 2 only

Verse

2nd time, Gtrs. 1 & 2: w/ Fill 1
2nd time, Gtr. 3: w/ Fill 1A

1. Con - ver - sion, __ soft - ware __ ver - sion __ sev - en-point - 0,
2. More wood for their __ fi - res _____ loud neigh - bors, __

look - ing at life through the eyes of a ti - re hub. __
flash - light rev-er-ies caught in the head - lights _____ of a truck.

Eat - ing seeds _____ as a pas - time _____ ac - tiv - i - ty,

the tox - ic - i - ty _____ of our cit - y, _____ of our cit - y.

Chorus

1., 2. New!   What do you own the world?   How do you own dis - or - der, _____ dis - or - der.
3.   New!   What do you own the world?   How do you own dis - or - der. _____

Now!   Some-where be - tween the sa - cred si - lence, sa - cred si - lence and sleep. _____

Some - where _____ be - tween the sa - cred si - lence and sleep, dis

or - der, _____ dis - or - der, _____ dis - or - der. _____ Mm. _____

Mm. _____ or - der.

Interlude

Double time ♩ = 164

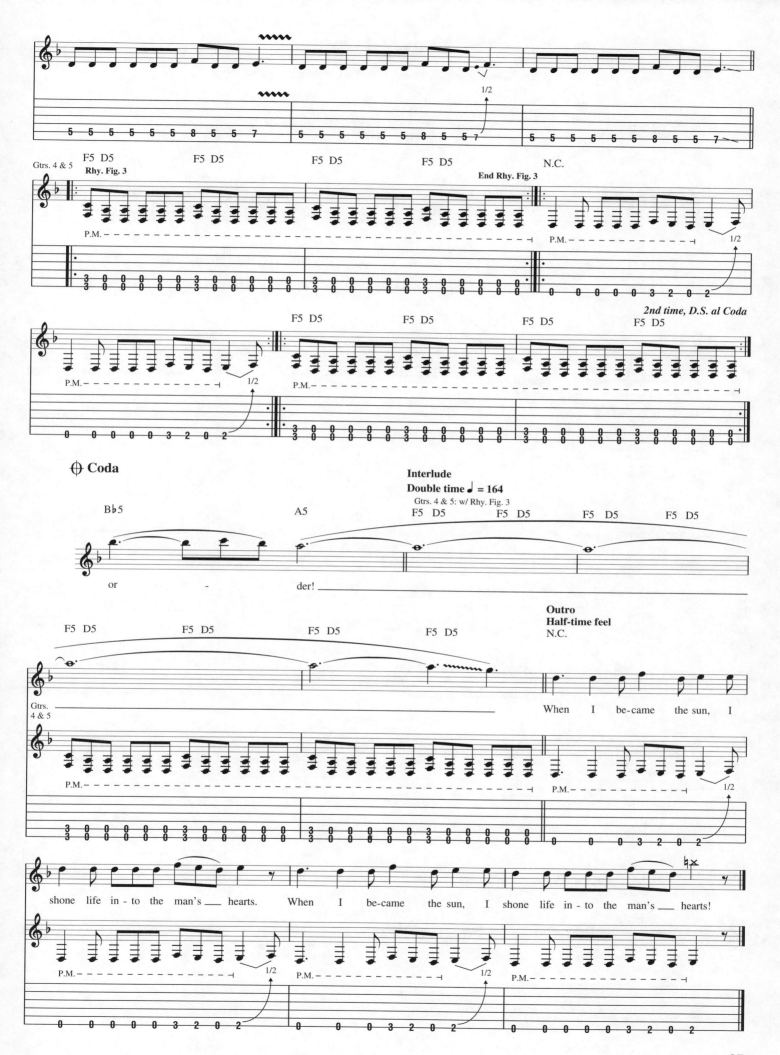

or - der!

When I be-came the sun, I shone life in-to the man's ___ hearts. When I be-came the sun, I shone life in-to the man's ___ hearts!

Psycho

Words and Music by Daron Malakian and Serj Tankian

Aerials

Words and Music by Daron Malakian and Serj Tankian

Gtrs. 1, 2 & 3: Drop D tuning, down 1 step:
(low to high) C–G–C–F–A–D

Gtr. 4: DADGAD tuning, down 1 step:
(low to high) C–G–C–F–G–C

Intro
Free time

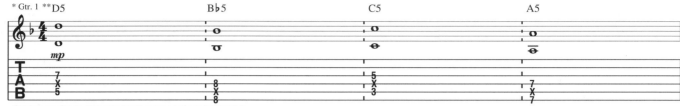

* Strings arr. for gtr. (1st notes begin over end of previous track.)

** Chord symbols reflect implied harmony.

Moderately fast ♩ = 162

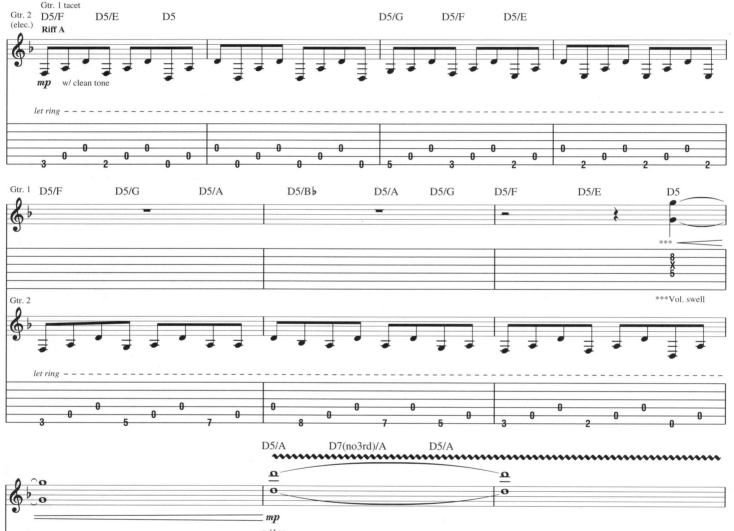

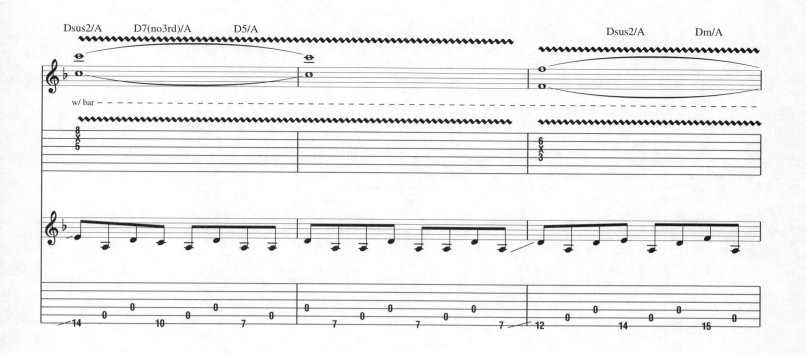

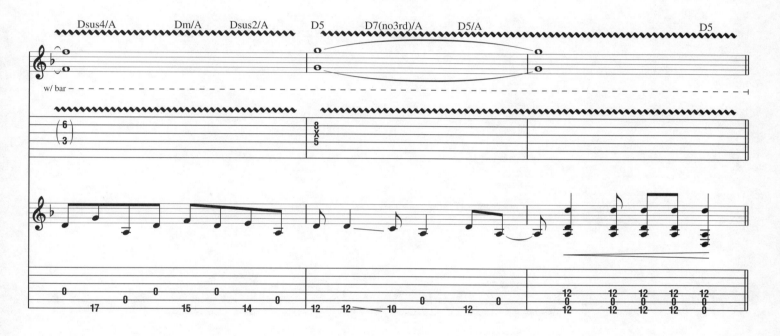

Verse

Half-time feel

Gtrs. 1 & 2 tacet
2nd time, Gtr. 4 tacet

1., 2. Life is a wa - ter - fall, __ we're one in the riv - er and one __ a - gain af - ter the fall. __
we drink from the riv - er, then we turn a - round and put up our walls. __

* Gtr. 3
(elec.) **Rhy. Fig. 1**

f w/ dist.

* Doubled throughout

Gtr. 3: w/ Rhy. Fig. 1 (2 1/2 times)

Bb5

Swim-ming through the void we hear ____ the word, ____ we lose our-selves ____ but we

D5   G5   D5   F5   D5   E5   D5

find it all. ____ 'Cause

Bb5

we are the ones that wan - na play, ____ al - ways wan - na go but you

D5   G5   D5   F5   D5   E5   D5

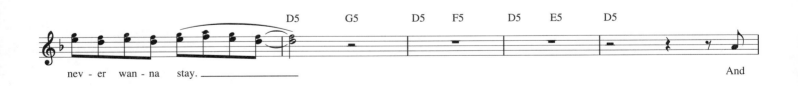

nev - er wan - na stay. ____ And

To Coda ⊕

Bb5

we are the ones that wan - na choose, ____ al - ways wan - na play but you nev - er wan - na lose. ____

Coda

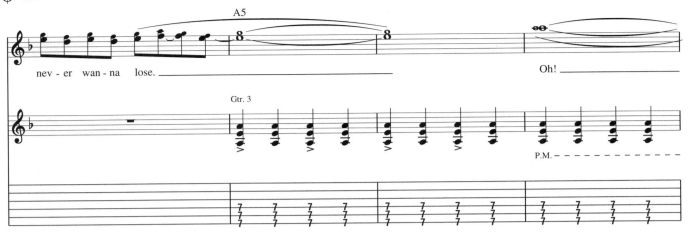

never wanna lose. Oh!

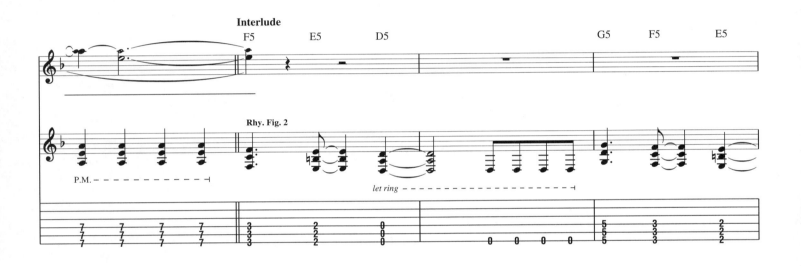

Interlude

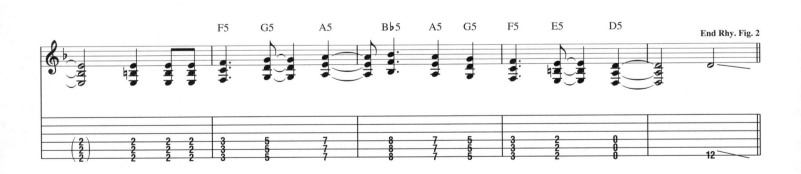

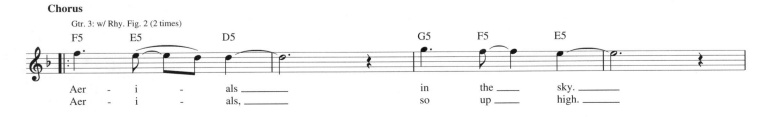

Chorus

Gtr. 3: w/ Rhy. Fig. 2 (2 times)

Aerials in the sky.
Aerials, so up high.

When you ___ lose ___ small ___ mind, you ___ free ___ your ___ life. ___
When you ___ free ___ your ___ eyes, e - ter - nal ___ prize. ___

Chorus

Gtrs. 2 & 4: w/ Riffs A & B (2 times)

Aer - i - als ___ in the ___ sky. ___
Aer - i - als, ___ so up ___ high. ___

When you ___ lose ___ small ___ mind, you ___ free ___ your ___ life. ___
When you ___ free ___ your ___ eyes, e - ter - nal ___ prize. ___

Outro

Gtrs. 2 & 4: w/ Riffs A & B (1 3/4 times)

Ah, ___ ah. ___ Ah. ___

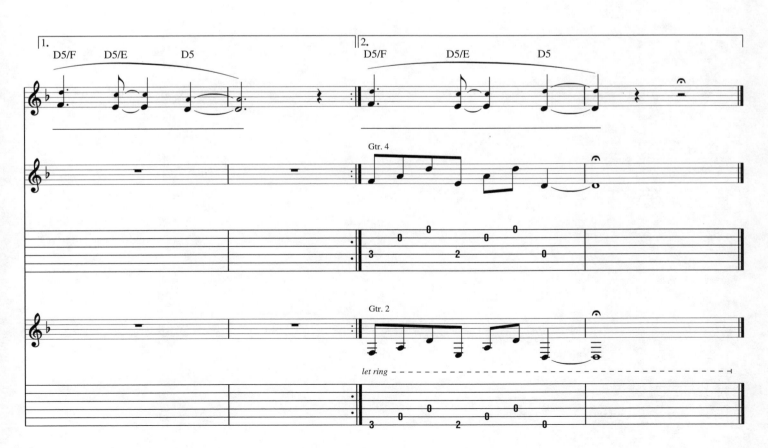

Guitar Notation Legend

Guitar Music can be notated three different ways: on a *musical staff*, in *tablature*, and in *rhythm slashes*.

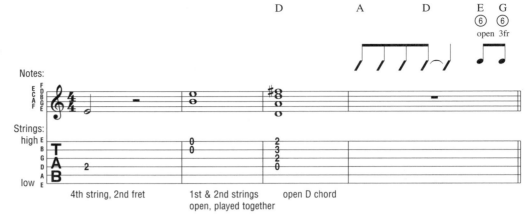

RHYTHM SLASHES are written above the staff. Strum chords in the rhythm indicated. Use the chord diagrams found at the top of the first page of the transcription for the appropriate chord voicings. Round noteheads indicate single notes.

THE MUSICAL STAFF shows pitches and rhythms and is divided by bar lines into measures. Pitches are named after the first seven letters of the alphabet.

TABLATURE graphically represents the guitar fingerboard. Each horizontal line represents a a string, and each number represents a fret.

Definitions for Special Guitar Notation

HALF-STEP BEND: Strike the note and bend up 1/2 step.

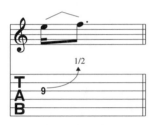

WHOLE-STEP BEND: Strike the note and bend up one step.

GRACE NOTE BEND: Strike the note and immediately bend up as indicated.

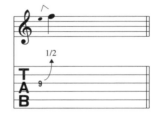

SLIGHT (MICROTONE) BEND: Strike the note and bend up 1/4 step.

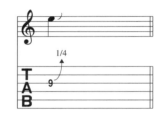

BEND AND RELEASE: Strike the note and bend up as indicated, then release back to the original note. Only the first note is struck.

PRE-BEND: Bend the note as indicated, then strike it.

PRE-BEND AND RELEASE: Bend the note as indicated. Strike it and release the bend back to the original note.

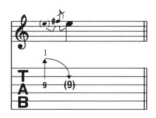

UNISON BEND: Strike the two notes simultaneously and bend the lower note up to the pitch of the higher.

VIBRATO: The string is vibrated by rapidly bending and releasing the note with the fretting hand.

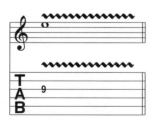

WIDE VIBRATO: The pitch is varied to a greater degree by vibrating with the fretting hand.

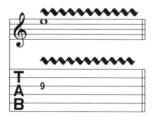

HAMMER-ON: Strike the first (lower) note with one finger, then sound the higher note (on the same string) with another finger by fretting it without picking.

PULL-OFF: Place both fingers on the notes to be sounded. Strike the first note and without picking, pull the finger off to sound the second (lower) note.

LEGATO SLIDE: Strike the first note and then slide the same fret-hand finger up or down to the second note. The second note is not struck.

SHIFT SLIDE: Same as legato slide, except the second note is struck.

TRILL: Very rapidly alternate between the notes indicated by continuously hammering on and pulling off.

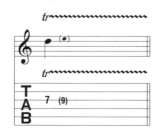

TAPPING: Hammer ("tap") the fret indicated with the pick-hand index or middle finger and pull off to the note fretted by the fret hand.

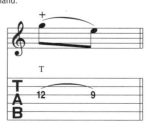

NATURAL HARMONIC: Strike the note while the fret-hand lightly touches the string directly over the fret indicated.

PINCH HARMONIC: The note is fretted normally and a harmonic is produced by adding the edge of the thumb or the tip of the index finger of the pick hand to the normal pick attack.

HARP HARMONIC: The note is fretted normally and a harmonic is produced by gently resting the pick hand's index finger directly above the indicated fret (in parentheses) while the pick hand's thumb or pick assists by plucking the appropriate string.

PICK SCRAPE: The edge of the pick is rubbed down (or up) the string, producing a scratchy sound.

MUFFLED STRINGS: A percussive sound is produced by laying the fret hand across the string(s) without depressing, and striking them with the pick hand.

PALM MUTING: The note is partially muted by the pick hand lightly touching the string(s) just before the bridge.

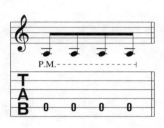

RAKE: Drag the pick across the strings indicated with a single motion.

TREMOLO PICKING: The note is picked as rapidly and continuously as possible.

ARPEGGIATE: Play the notes of the chord indicated by quickly rolling them from bottom to top.

VIBRATO BAR DIVE AND RETURN: The pitch of the note or chord is dropped a specified number of steps (in rhythm) then returned to the original pitch.

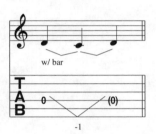

VIBRATO BAR SCOOP: Depress the bar just before striking the note, then quickly release the bar.

VIBRATO BAR DIP: Strike the note and then immediately drop a specified number of steps, then release back to the original pitch.

Additional Musical Definitions

Symbol	Term	Description
(accent)		• Accentuate note (play it louder)
(accent)		• Accentuate note with great intensity
(staccato)		• Play the note short
⊓		• Downstroke
∨		• Upstroke
D.S. al Coda		• Go back to the sign (𝄋), then play until the measure marked "**To Coda**," then skip to the section labelled "**Coda**."
D.C. al Fine		• Go back to the beginning of the song and play until the measure marked "***Fine***" (end).

Rhy. Fig. • Label used to recall a recurring accompaniment pattern (usually chordal).

Riff • Label used to recall composed, melodic lines (usually single notes) which recur.

Fill • Label used to identify a brief melodic figure which is to be inserted into the arrangement.

Rhy. Fill • A chordal version of a Fill.

tacet • Instrument is silent (drops out).

 • Repeat measures between signs.

 • When a repeated section has different endings, play the first ending only the first time and the second ending only the second time.

NOTE: Tablature numbers in parentheses mean:
1. The note is being sustained over a system (note in standard notation is tied), or
2. The note is sustained, but a new articulation (such as a hammer-on, pull-off, slide or vibrato begins), or
3. The note is a barely audible "ghost" note (note in standard notation is also in parentheses).

RECORDED VERSIONS
GUITAR
The Best Note-For-Note Transcriptions Available

ALL BOOKS INCLUDE TABLATURE

00690016 Will Ackerman Collection $19.95	00690127 Goo Goo Dolls – A Boy Named Goo $19.95	00690395 Rage Against The Machine –
00690146 Aerosmith – Toys in the Attic $19.95	00690338 Goo Goo Dolls – Dizzy Up the Girl $19.95	The Battle of Los Angeles $19.95
00694865 Alice In Chains – Dirt $19.95	00690117 John Gorka Collection $19.95	00690145 Rage Against The Machine – Evil Empire ..$19.95
00694932 Allman Brothers Band – Volume 1 .....$24.95	00690114 Buddy Guy Collection Vol. A-J $22.95	00690179 Rancid – And Out Come the Wolves $22.95
00694933 Allman Brothers Band – Volume 2 .....$24.95	00690193 Buddy Guy Collection Vol. L-Y $22.95	00690055 Red Hot Chili Peppers –
00694934 Allman Brothers Band – Volume 3 .....$24.95	00694798 George Harrison Anthology $19.95	Bloodsugarsexmagik $19.95
00694877 Chet Atkins – Guitars For All Seasons ...$19.95	00690068 Return Of The Hellecasters $19.95	00690379 Red Hot Chili Peppers – Californication ..$19.95
00690418 Best of Audio Adrenaline $17.95	00692930 Jimi Hendrix – Are You Experienced? ...$24.95	00690090 Red Hot Chili Peppers – One Hot Minute .$22.95
00694918 Randy Bachman Collection $22.95	00692931 Jimi Hendrix – Axis: Bold As Love $22.95	00694937 Jimmy Reed – Master Bluesman $19.95
00690366 Bad Company Original Anthology - Bk 1 .$19.95	00692932 Jimi Hendrix – Electric Ladyland $24.95	00694899 R.E.M. – Automatic For The People $19.95
00690367 Bad Company Original Anthology - Bk 2 .$19.95	00690218 Jimi Hendrix – First Rays of the New Rising Sun $27.95	00690260 Jimmie Rodgers Guitar Collection $19.95
00694880 Beatles – Abbey Road $19.95	00690038 Gary Hoey – Best Of $19.95	00690014 Rolling Stones – Exile On Main Street ..$24.95
00694863 Beatles –	00660029 Buddy Holly $19.95	00690186 Rolling Stones – Rock & Roll Circus ...$19.95
Sgt. Pepper's Lonely Hearts Club Band ..$19.95	00660169 John Lee Hooker – A Blues Legend $19.95	00690135 Otis Rush Collection $19.95
00690383 Beatles – Yellow Submarine $19.95	00690054 Hootie & The Blowfish –	00690031 Santana's Greatest Hits $19.95
00690174 Beck – Mellow Gold $17.95	Cracked Rear View $19.95	00690150 Son Seals – Bad Axe Blues $17.95
00690346 Beck – Mutations $19.95	00694905 Howlin' Wolf $19.95	00690128 Seven Mary Three – American Standards .$19.95
00690175 Beck – Odelay $17.95	00690136 Indigo Girls – 1200 Curfews $22.95	00120105 Kenny Wayne Shepherd – Ledbetter Heights $19.95
00694884 The Best of George Benson $19.95	00694938 Elmore James –	00120123 Kenny Wayne Shepherd – Trouble Is ...$19.95
00692385 Chuck Berry $19.95	Master Electric Slide Guitar $19.95	00690196 Silverchair – Freak Show $19.95
00692200 Black Sabbath –	00690167 Skip James Blues Guitar Collection ...$16.95	00690130 Silverchair – Frogstomp $19.95
We Sold Our Soul For Rock 'N' Roll $19.95	00694833 Billy Joel For Guitar $19.95	00690041 Smithereens – Best Of $19.95
00690115 Blind Melon – Soup $19.95	00694912 Eric Johnson – Ah Via Musicom $19.95	00690385 Sonicflood $19.95
00690305 Blink 182 – Dude Ranch $19.95	00690169 Eric Johnson – Venus Isle $22.95	00694885 Spin Doctors – Pocket Full Of Kryptonite $19.95
00690028 Blue Oyster Cult – Cult Classics $19.95	00694799 Robert Johnson – At The Crossroads ...$19.95	00694921 Steppenwolf, The Best Of $22.95
00690219 Blur $19.95	00693185 Judas Priest – Vintage Hits $19.95	00694957 Rod Stewart – Acoustic Live $22.95
00690168 Roy Buchanon Collection $19.95	00690277 Best of Kansas $19.95	00690021 Sting – Fields Of Gold $19.95
00690364 Cake – Songbook $19.95	00690073 B. B. King – 1950-1957 ....$24.95	00690242 Suede – Coming Up $19.95
00690337 Jerry Cantrell – Boggy Depot $19.95	00690098 B. B. King – 1958-1967 ....$24.95	00694824 Best Of James Taylor $16.95
00690293 Best of Steven Curtis Chapman $19.95	00690444 B.B. King and Eric Clapton –	00690238 Third Eye Blind $19.95
00690043 Cheap Trick – Best Of $19.95	Riding with the King $19.95	00690403 Third Eye Blind – Blue $19.95
00690171 Chicago – Definitive Guitar Collection ...$22.95	00690134 Freddie King Collection $17.95	00690267 311 ....$19.95
00690415 Clapton Chronicles – Best of Eric Clapton .$17.95	00690157 Kiss – Alive $19.95	00690030 Toad The Wet Sprocket $19.95
00690393 Eric Clapton – Selections from Blues ...$19.95	00690163 Mark Knopfler/Chet Atkins – Neck and Neck $19.95	00690228 Tonic – Lemon Parade $19.95
00660139 Eric Clapton – Journeyman $19.95	00690296 Patty Larkin Songbook $17.95	00690295 Tool – Aenima $19.95
00694869 Eric Clapton – Live Acoustic $19.95	00690018 Living Colour – Best Of $19.95	00690039 Steve Vai – Alien Love Secrets $24.95
00694896 John Mayall/Eric Clapton – Bluesbreakers $19.95	00694845 Yngwie Malmsteen – Fire And Ice $19.95	00690172 Steve Vai – Fire Garden $24.95
00690162 Best of the Clash $19.95	00694956 Bob Marley – Legend $19.95	00690023 Jimmie Vaughan – Strange Pleasures ...$19.95
00690166 Albert Collins – The Alligator Years $16.95	00690283 Best of Sarah McLachlan $19.95	00690370 Stevie Ray Vaughan and Double Trouble –
00694940 Counting Crows – August & Everything After $19.95	00690382 Sarah McLachlan – Mirrorball $19.95	The Real Deal: Greatest Hits Volume 2 ...$22.95
00690197 Counting Crows – Recovering the Satellites .$19.95	00690354 Sarah McLachlan – Surfacing $19.95	00690455 Stevie Ray Vaughan – Blues at Sunrise ...$19.95
00694840 Cream – Disraeli Gears $19.95	00690442 Matchbox 20 – Mad Season $19.95	00660136 Stevie Ray Vaughan – In Step $19.95
00690401 Creed – Human Clay $19.95	00690239 Matchbox 20 – Yourself or Someone Like You $19.95	00694817 Stevie Ray Vaughan – Live at Carnegie Hall $19.95
00690352 Creed – My Own Prison $19.95	00690244 Megadeath – Cryptic Writings $19.95	00694835 Stevie Ray Vaughan – The Sky Is Crying .$19.95
00690184 dc Talk – Jesus Freak $19.95	00690236 Mighty Mighty Bosstones – Let's Face It .$19.95	00694776 Vaughan Brothers – Family Style $19.95
00690333 dc Talk – Supernatural $19.95	00690040 Steve Miller Band Greatest Hits $19.95	00120026 Joe Walsh – Look What I Did... ......$24.95
00660186 Alex De Grassi Guitar Collection $19.95	00694802 Gary Moore – Still Got The Blues $19.95	00694789 Muddy Waters – Deep Blues $24.95
00690289 Best of Deep Purple $17.95	00694958 Mountain, Best Of $19.95	00690071 Weezer $19.95
00694831 Derek And The Dominos –	00690448 MxPx – The Ever Passing Moment $19.95	00690286 Weezer – Pinkerton $19.95
Layla & Other Assorted Love Songs $19.95	00694913 Nirvana – In Utero $19.95	00690447 Who, The – Best of $24.95
00690322 Ani Di Franco – Little Plastic Castle $19.95	00694883 Nirvana – Nevermind $19.95	00694970 Who, The – Definitive Collection A-E ..$24.95
00690187 Dire Straits – Brothers In Arms $19.95	00690026 Nirvana – Acoustic In New York $19.95	00694971 Who, The – Definitive Collection F-Li ..$24.95
00690191 Dire Straits – Money For Nothing $24.95	00690121 Oasis – (What's The Story) Morning Glory .$19.95	00694972 Who, The – Definitive Collection Lo-R ..$24.95
00695382 The Very Best of Dire Straits –	00690204 Offspring, The – Ixnay on the Hombre ...$17.95	00694973 Who, The – Definitive Collection S-Y ...$24.95
Sultans of Swing $19.95	00690203 Offspring, The – Smash $17.95	00690319 Stevie Wonder Hits $17.95
00660178 Willie Dixon – Master Blues Composer ..$24.95	00694830 Ozzy Osbourne – No More Tears $19.95	
00690250 Best of Duane Eddy $16.95	00694855 Pearl Jam – Ten $19.95	
00690349 Eve 6 ....$19.95	00690053 Liz Phair – Whip Smart $19.95	
00313164 Eve 6 – Horrorscope $19.95	00690176 Phish – Billy Breathes $22.95	
00690323 Fastball – All the Pain Money Can Buy ..$19.95	00690424 Phish – Farmhouse $19.95	
00690089 Foo Fighters $19.95	00690331 Phish – The Story of Ghost $19.95	
00690235 Foo Fighters – The Colour and the Shape .$19.95	00690428 Pink Floyd – Dark Side of the Moon ...$19.95	
00690394 Foo Fighters –	00693800 Pink Floyd – Early Classics $19.95	
There Is Nothing Left to Lose $19.95	00690456 P.O.D. – The Fundamental	
00690222 G3 Live – Satriani, Vai, Johnson $22.95	Elements of Southtown $19.95	
00694807 Danny Gatton – 88 Elmira St $19.95	00694967 Police – Message In A Box Boxed Set ...$70.00	
00690438 Genesis Guitar Anthology $19.95	00694974 Queen – A Night At The Opera $19.95